Jewish Folk and Holiday Songs

Easy Edition

Arranged by WESLEY SCHAUM

for Piano or Electronic Keyboard

Music consultant ALFRED CAHN

Editorial suggestions by Cantor Roy Garber and Mrs. Nathan Slutzky
Transliteration by Miriam Ben-Shemuel

FOREWORD

These revered Jewish Folk and Holiday Songs have been simplified so that they are easily playable by most students. Respectful arrangements retain the traditional character of the music. This collection is intended for all types of youth and adult Jewish organizations, clubs and groups.

The selections are mainly in Hebrew in either the Ashkenazic or the Sephardic dialect. There are also a few songs in Yiddish and English.

The classifications on page 2 list the most common usage of the music. However, most of the pieces may be used for more than one occasion and are not necessarily restricted to the use listed.

The music portrays a wide range of emotions subject to individual interpretation. The performer is free to play at different tempos or with rubato, according to personal taste. Likewise, dynamic inflections and pedaling may be added or altered.

A *pronunciation guide* appears on page 2.

Translation of the Lyrics is on page 24.

Schaum Publications, Inc.
10235 N. Port Washington Rd. • Mequon, WI 53092 • www.schaumpiano.net

ISBN-13: 978-1-936098-04-0

09-46

Contents

Pronunciation Guide

Sound	Example in text	English Equivalent
a	sh<u>a</u>	f<u>a</u>ther
ay	<u>ay</u>n	m<u>i</u>ne
e	n<u>e</u>	h<u>e</u>n
ee	sh<u>ee</u>	f<u>ee</u>l
ey	l<u>ey</u>	l<u>ay</u>
i	t<u>i</u>k	w<u>i</u>t
i	l<u>i</u>	l<u>ee</u>
o	l<u>o</u>m	h<u>u</u>m
o	n<u>o</u>	g<u>o</u>
oo	h<u>oo</u>	r<u>oo</u>m
oy	<u>oy</u>	j<u>oy</u>
u	z<u>u</u>m	r<u>oo</u>m

Consonants are same as in English, except those indicated below:

ch	<u>ch</u>ad	Ba<u>ch</u>
g	<u>g</u>i	<u>g</u>ift

Note: There is no standardization of the Hebrew transliteration and this Pronunciation Guide is only a general aid.

Translation of the lyrics
is on page 24

Hatikvah

* Use of pedal is optional throughout the book.

Hevenu Shalom Aleychem

Allegretto ♩= 116-120

Sabbath Greeting Song

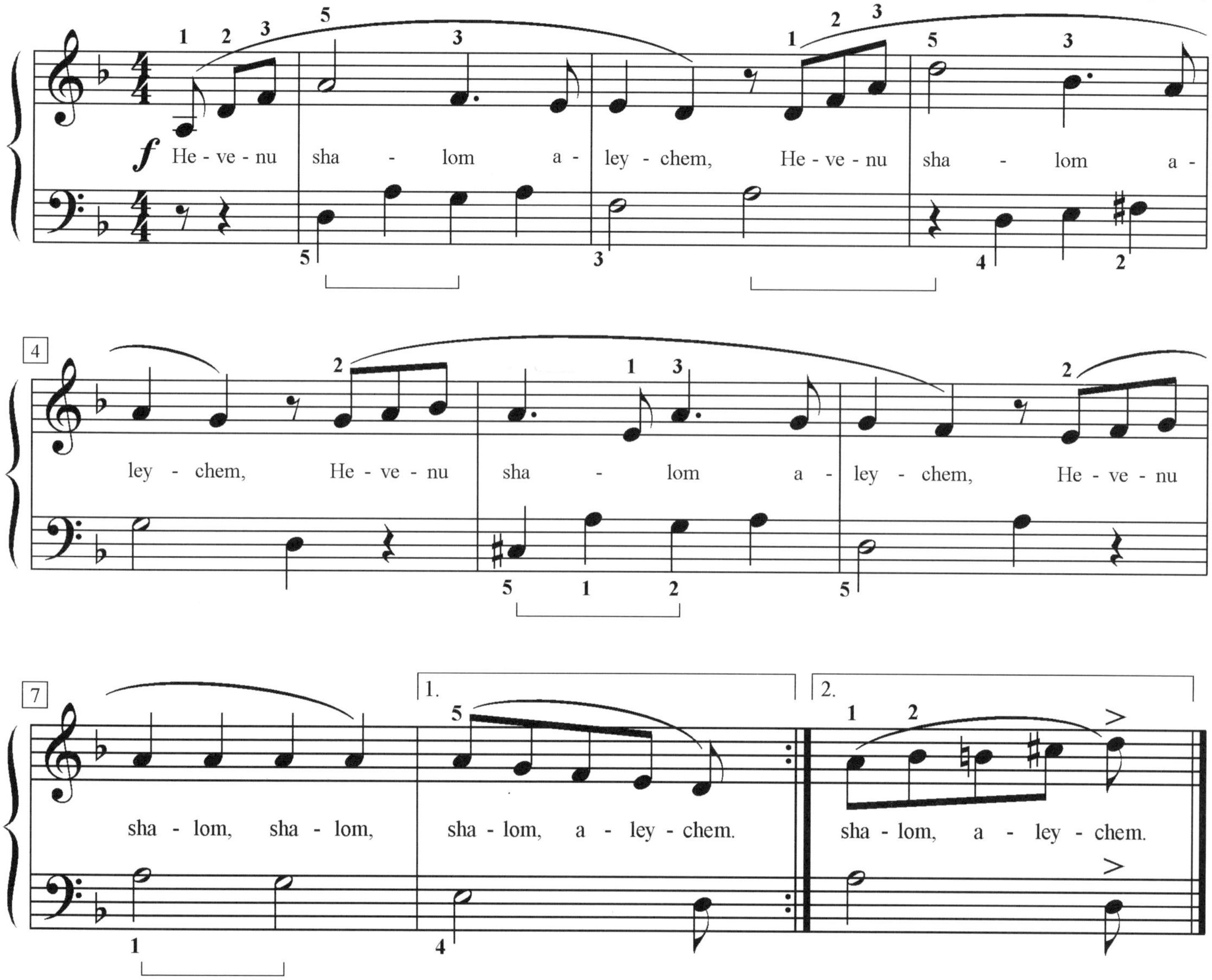

Artza Alinu

Moderato ♩= 112-120

Folk Dance

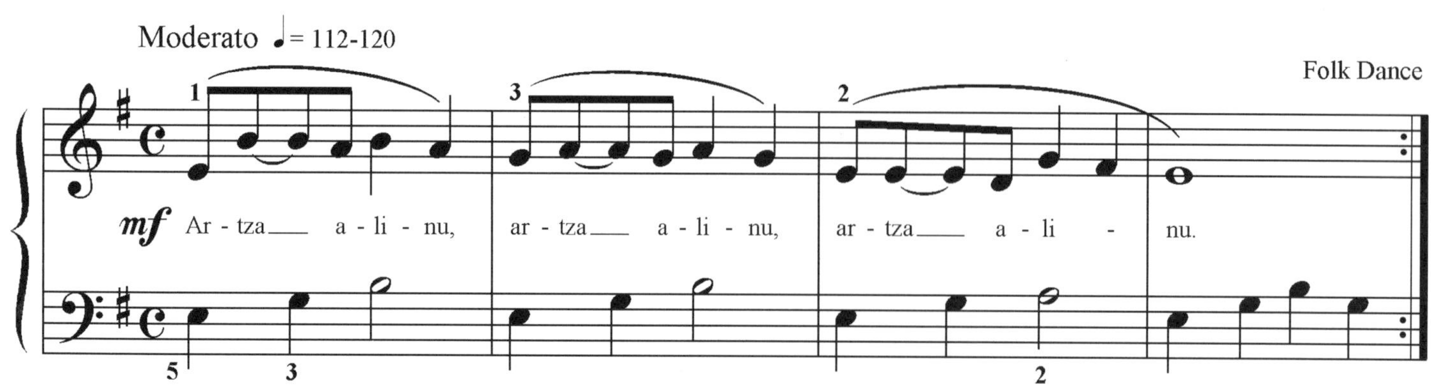

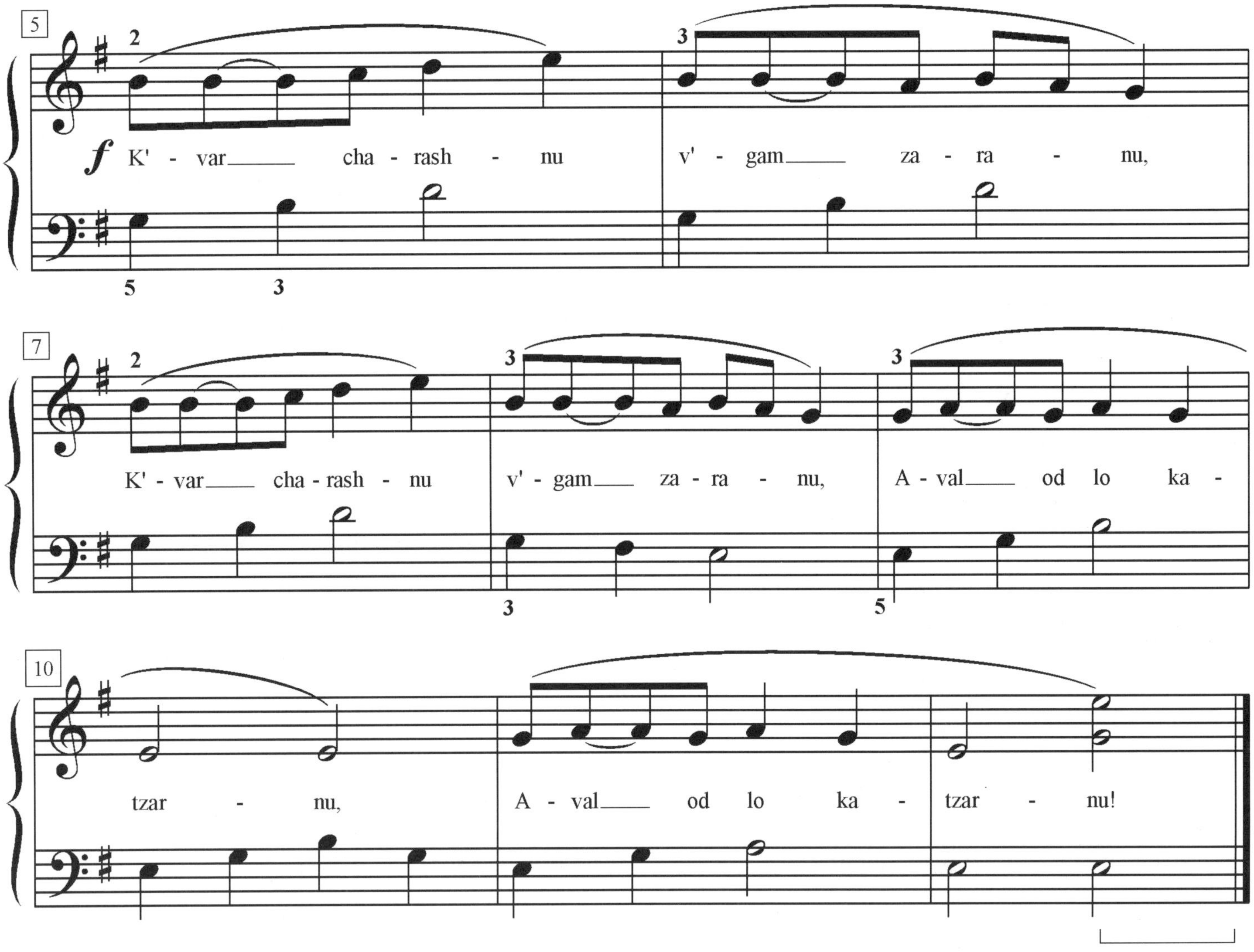

Shalom Chaveyreem

Moderato ♩ = 116-126

Folk Song

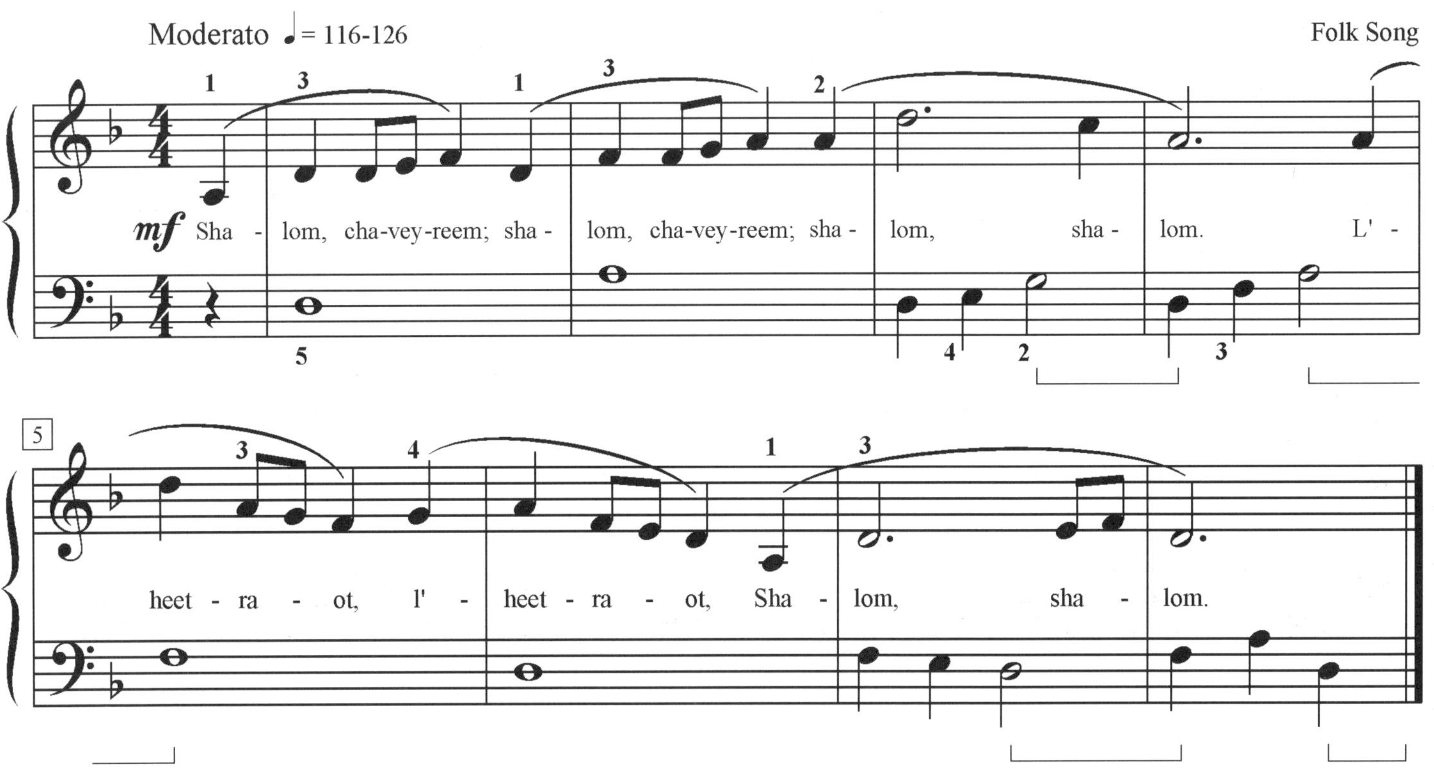

Hava Nagila

Allegro ♩= 112-120
Israeli Folk Song
mf Ha - va na - gi - la, Ha - va na - gi - la,
Ha - va na - gi - la, v' - nis - m' - cha.
Ha - va n' - ra - ne - nah, Ha - va n' - ra - ne - nah,
Ha - va n' - ra - ne - nah, v' - nis - m' - cha.
mp U - - - ru, cresc. U - ru a - chim,

Uru a - chim b' - lev sa - mey - ach, Uru a - chim b' - lev sa - mey - ach,
Uru a - chim b' - lev sa - mey - ach, Uru a - chim b' - lev sa - mey - ach,
Uru a - chim, Uru a - chim, b'lev sa - mey - ach.
Ha - va na - gi - la, Ha - va na - gi - la,
Ha - va na - gi - la, v' - nis - m' - cha.

Zum Gali Gali

Lama Suka Zu

Andante ♩ = 72-76
Folk Song
mp
La - ma su - ka zu,   A - ba tov she - li?
La - ma su - ka zu,   A - ba tov she - li?   Ley -
shev ba - su - ka, ya - ki - ri, Ley - shev ba - su - ka, cha - vi - vi, Ley -
shev ba - su - ka, ye - led cheyn,   Ye - led cheyn she - li.   Ley -
shev ba - su - ka, ye - led cheyn,   Ye - led cheyn she - li.

Eli, Eli

Moderato ♩ = 120-126
Traditional Yiddish Folk Song
mp
Eli, Eli, la - ma a - sav - ta - nu? E - li, E - li, la - ma a - sav - ta - nu? Mit Fei - er und Flam hat men uns ge - brent i - ber - al hat men uns ge - macht zu Schand, zu
mf

Mazel Tov

Allegro ♩ = 120-126

Traditional Yiddish

Avinu Malkeynu

Kol Nidrey

Lento e rubato ♩ = 72-76
Traditional
Words from the Liturgy
Piu mosso ♩ = 138
Lento e rubato ♩ = 72-76
p
Kol nid - rey ve - e - so - rey va - cha - ro - mey ve - ko - no-
mey ve - chi - nu -yey v' - ki - nu - sey u - sh'vu - os.
mp
Kol nid - rey ve - e - so - rey va - cha - ro mey ve - ko - no-
rit.
mey ve - chi - nu -yey v' - ki - nu - sey u - sh'vu - os.

Rock of Ages
(Mo-oz Tzur)

* The English lyrics are not an exact translation.

Chanuka Oy Chanuka

Chanuka Song

Traditional
English words by E. Fragen

Purim Day
(Chag Purim)

Eliyahu Hanavi

Go Down Moses

Chad Gadya

Andantino ♩ = 92-100
Traditional
Chad gad - ya, Chad gad - ya. De - za - bin a - ba bit - rey zu - zey,
Chad gad - ya, Chad gad - ya. Ve - a - ta shun - ra ve - a - chal le - gad - ye, De -
za - bin a - ba bit - rey zu - zey, Chad gad - ya, Chad gad - ya. Ve -
a - ta kal - ba ve - na - shach le - shun - ra De - a - chal le - gad - ya. De -
za - bin a - ba bit - rey zu - zey, Chad gad - ya, Chad gad - ya.
mf
mp
mf
rit.

Boruch Eloheynu

Eyn Keyloheynu

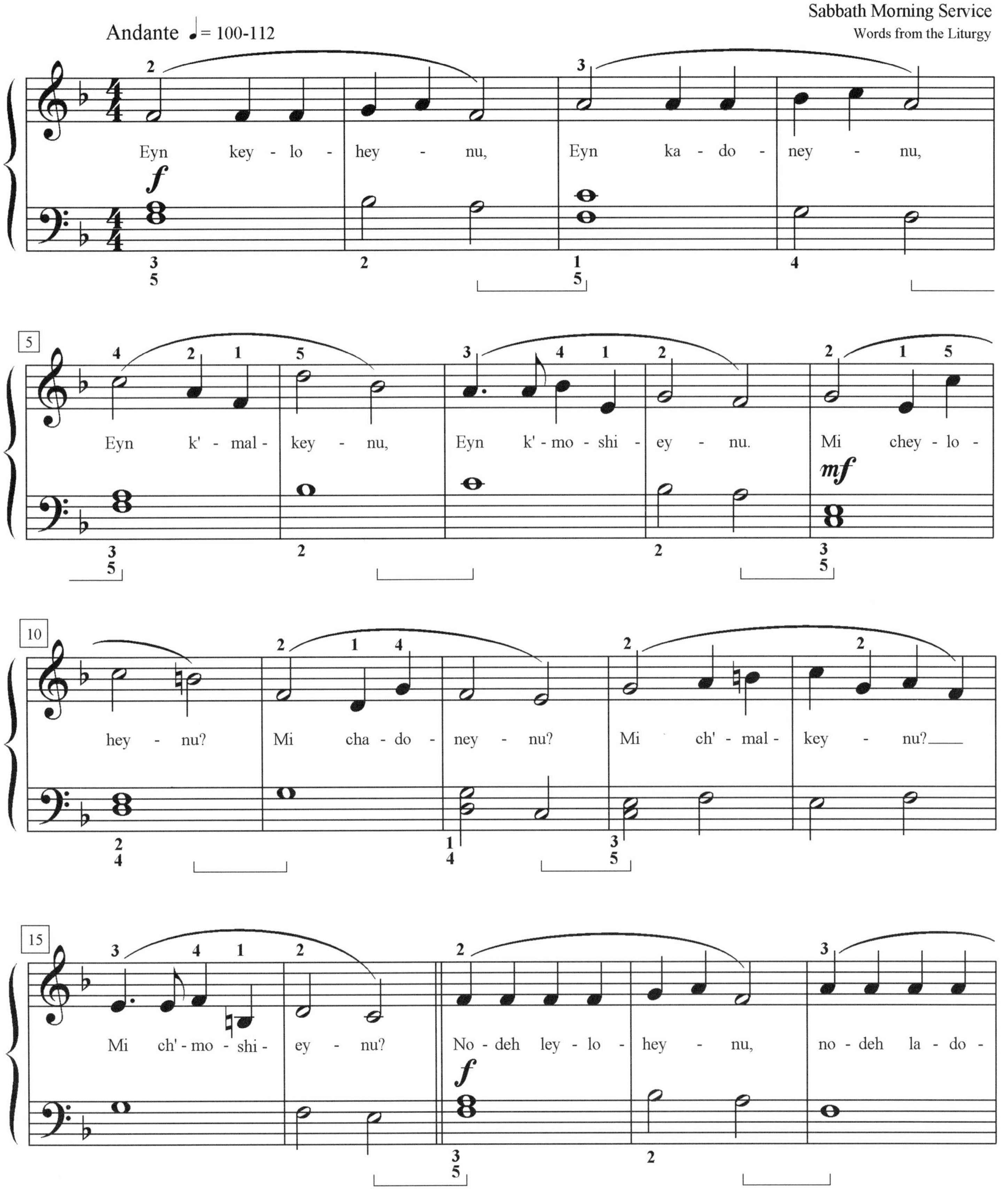

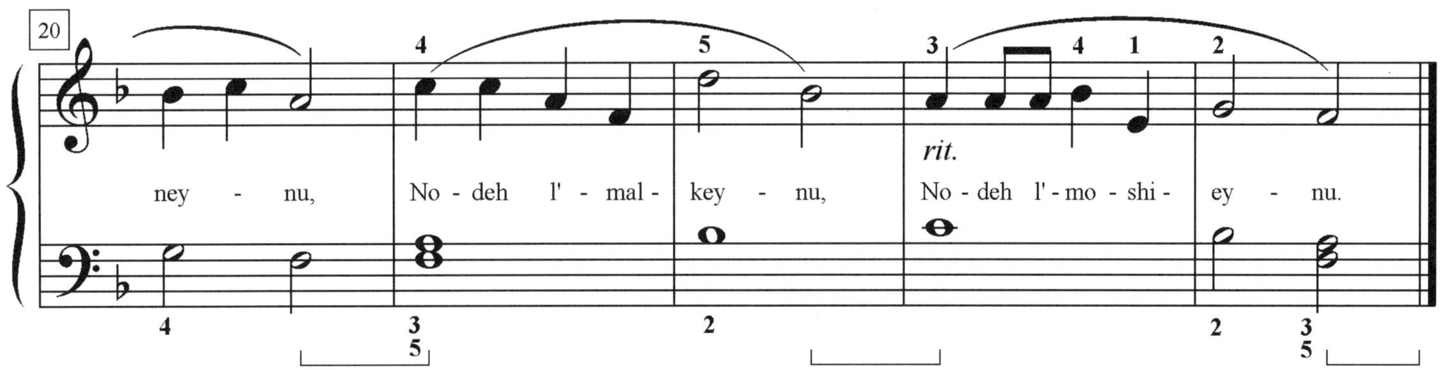

Adon Olam

Traditional
Words from the Liturgy

Allegretto ♩ = 104-112

Translation of the Lyrics

by Miriam Ben-Shemuel and Alfred Cahn

> The intent of these translations is to provide an understanding of the meaning of the lyrics. The translations are not literal and therefore, will not fit with the music.

Hatikvah (page 3)

As long as there, deep in the heart, a Jewish soul
is vibrating, Our hope is not lost yet:
To be a free people in our land, the land of Zion
and Jerusalem.

Hevenu Shalom Aleychem (page 4)

We brought peace upon you.

Artza Alinu (page 4)

We ascended upon the land.
We already plowed and sowed,
But we have not harvested yet.

Shalom Chaveyreem (page 5)

Peace, comrades. See you again!

Hava Nagila (page 6)

Let's rejoice,
Let's sing and let's be happy.
Utter a song, brothers, with a happy heart.

Zum Gali Gali (page 8)

["Zum Gali Gali" cannot be translated. It is equivalent
to a humming sound and has no other meaning.
The last two lines translate as:]

The pioneer is made for work.
The work is made for the pioneer

Lama Suka Zu (page 9)

[This song is sung during the Festival of the Tabernacles
when Jews pray and eat their meals in a flimsy hut, covered
with twigs and leaves, and decorated inside with the fruit and
harvest of the land: The first Thanksgiving
celebration in recorded history!]

Why this booth, my good father?
To sit in the booth, my dear one.
Our forefathers did it and so do we.
To sit in the booth, my loving-one,
To sit in the booth, charming lad, my charming boy,
To sit in the booth, charming lad, my charming boy.

Eli, Eli (page 10) [Line 2 and after is Yiddish]

My God, my God, why have You forsaken us?
With fire and flames they have burnt us.
Everywhere they have disgraced and derided us;
But none of us ventured to deviate from our holy
Torah, our Commandments.

Mazel Tov (page 11) [Yiddish]

Good luck to groom and bride.
We sing to all, a good holiday today.

Avinu Malkeynu (page 12)

[This is only a small part of a solemn prayer.]
Our Father, our King, be gracious and answer us,
for we have little merit.
Treat us generously and with kindness,
and be our Saviour.

Kol Nidrey (page 13)

[This prayer is one of the most solemn recited on the
eve of Yom Kippur (Day of Awe), and is in the Aramaic
dialect spoken more than 2000 years ago, when the
Jews were in exile in Babylon. The music is an abbreviated
version. The text translates as:]

All vows, oaths and promises which we
made to God should be annulled.

[The seeming contradiction of the lyrics has created
questions as to their origin and meaning as well as
ethical and religious-legal problems. Rabbis have
established strict conditions on annulments involving
investigation and deliberation by a religious court or
scholarly authority.
   Persecutions and forced conversion to Christianity
in Spain during the 6th and 7th century and later during
the Inquisition may have been the reason for the lyrics.]

Chanuka, Oy Chanuka (page 15) [Yiddish]

O Chanuka, O Chanuka, a beautiful holiday,
A merry one, a joyous one. There is none like it.
Every night we play the dreidel,*
and eat hot potato pancakes with no limit.
Children are in a hurry to light the thin candles.
Sing about the miracles, praise God for the miracles
and let us all dance.

*[A dreidel is a four-sided spinning top used in a
Chanuka game.]

Eliyahu Hanavi (page 18)

Elijah, the Prophet; Elijah the Tishbeite
Will speedily come with the Messiah, Son of David.

Chad Gadya (page 20)

One only kid [a young goat], one only kid
My father bought for two zoozim [ancient coin]
One only kid, one only kid.

[There are many additional verses.]

Boruch Eloheynu (page 21)

Blessed be our God who created us to His honor.
Once more and once more to His honor.

Eyn Keyloheynu (page 22)

There is none like our God,
There is none like our Master.
There is none like our King,
There is none like our Saviour.
Who is like our God? Who is like our Master?
Who is like our King? Who is like our Saviour?
We will thank our God. We will thank our Master.
We will thank our King. We will thank our Saviour.

Adon Olam (page 23)

Master of the world who ruled before any creature
was created.
He was called King at the time He was making
everything according to His will.